Circle of Ecstasy

Circle of Ecstasy

A Haiku Neophyte at 76

Antonio S. Dimalanta, MD

CIRCLE OF ECSTASY

First edition. January 12, 2023.

Copyright © 2023 Antonio S. Dimalanta.

ISBN: 9798215866085

Written by Antonio S. Dimalanta.

To You

Who took on the physical form to experience the ecstasy and sorrow of humanness, manifest and share Eternal/Infinite Love.

Acknowledgment

I am grateful for the inspiration, support, love, prayers, and greetings from my Centennial USTMED71 Classmates—especially the active members of our Messenger group. I can't list all 321, however; I recorded the Planning Committee members who do the tireless work of love and service: Agapito Valencia, MD, Erlinda Bayaua-Berendi, MD, Daniel Aguila, Jr, MD, Alice Mangalindan-Lim, MD, Shirley Villarica-Salvatierra, MD, Antonio Ong, MD, Lina Baraceros-Bouffard, MD, and Elpidio Mariano, MD provides the Messenger platform.

I admire the following loving, compassionate healers, artists, and beings.

Angela M. Sims, Ph.D., a Clinical Psychologist
Maria Loida Bernabe, MD, an Internist/Pediatrician,
Mrs. Myrna Bituin, an Entrepreneur and Environmentalist
Anselma Loredo-Canlas, MD, an Anesthesiologist
Stephanie Stenger, a Real Estate Lawyer
Mon David, an International Jazz Singer
Chloe D. Stenger, my Poet, granddaughter
My patients taught me about suffering and humanness.

A central group of my COE and 1000 daily gratitude is my wife, Flor; my kids and their partners: Jon/Angie, Arlene/Stu, and Abigail; my in-laws, Ron and Lezah Stenger, Ray and Becky Irby and their Families; my grandchildren: Anthony, Aubrey, Colin, Annabel, Chloe, and Grayson.

Contents

Introduction

What Am I Doing Here?

I asked myself: What am I doing here, writing Haiku, as reported in an article by Clark Strand in Tricycle Magazine in; Spring 2021 as The World's Most Popular Poem? It originated in Japan as a three-line 5-7-5, or seventeen syllables poem, which gained mainstream recognition in English speaking world in the early 20th century, in the UK, then in America, and now in the world.

In many languages, traditional Haiku poets still follow the formal convention, but modern poets write Haiku without the restrictive format. The brevity provides a challenge to capture an inspirational moment and a relief from a long-drawn poem with meters and rhymes. Words are abstracted things that make an encounter a meta-level to the actual incident and often get a sense of distance, differentiation from an illumination in a moment in time, Oneness with the object, the spirit, or God, The Source, Primordial or Pure Consciousness(PC).

Haiku Neophyte at 76

I was born in the Philippines and migrated to the United States in 1973. We used English as the primary language in the schools. We have over 180 dialects, and each one is a different language. Besides, we speak Taglish, a contract, combined or mixed English, and our national language, Tagalog. I don't recall any poetry Class and, indeed, no poem writing. We studied grammar, not phonetics, not idioms. I was more familiar with slapstick humor. It took me about three years to smile, let alone laugh at Johnny Carson's jokes.

At 31 years old, in 1977, I had my first of three spontaneous Satori, Samadhi, or Transcendence(SST) with the sunlight, which in a moment, totally and irreversibly changed my fundamental beliefs and being. The second was a fusion with darkness, and the third was a rebirth from two amorphous clouds that fused; I also had an Out of Body Experience(OBE) of symbolic death. I wrote a few simple poems to capture and relive a moment of Oneness with PC and the overwhelming ecstasy.

I do not know Haiku. I discovered it on January 12, a day before turning 76, after reading a short article sent by Grammarly on how to write poems. I wrote two poems on a whim and shared them in our Messenger group of Santo Tomas 1971 Doctor of Medicine Graduates.

Haiku knows me. Over four hundred poems in four months, coming out of my ears. A slice of a room is a thousand Haiku, and everything is alive, full of images, moments, and personalized things("Thingies"), lining up, wanting communion, and manifested. Then delightful unfolding processes, functions, forms, ease, comfort, peace, and Zen moments of bliss or a leap; are suspended in eternity.

431. Step on Haiku road

I couldn't get off the path

Maybe, none is real by purist standards or by Matsuo Basho, who said: "He who creates three to five haiku poems during a lifetime is a haiku poet. He who attains to complete ten is a master." Then again, what are the 17th to 21st-century criteria? Do evolution and impermanence make Basho's declaration outdated, static, distinctive, personal, or a misguided purism?

261. Basho's grass sandals

Seventeenth-century trips

Four-wheel drive gas truck

Purism is like perfection, a form of sickness! The only pure purity is never about purity because the metaphoric absurdity is, once put down on paper, spoken, conceptualized, or thought of, they are part of creation, separateness or differentiations that makes PC invisible as a transformation to concrete/matter, abstract/symbolic or metaphysical/spiritual occurs. Still, I had communion moments with PC and nature, presently written as Haiku.

The ideal event is that every moment is an SST; every task is a soul encounter and a communion with the divine--a Oneness with PC. The breakthrough to the divine realm is what Basho referred to as the extreme difficulty of creating a real Haiku, possibly not the poem itself, written from memory or mental design.

Haiku for a Beginner/Newoldkid

My life after SST is Zen, Buddhist, Catholic, Doctor, and layman. Buddhism has more mental components than The Wow moment of Zen with minimal intentional abstraction. My Catholic ways are towards a virtuous lifestyle.

I like oxymorons, merisms, conflicting, contradictory, inconsistent, paradoxical, funny, and absurd combinations of words. They frequently are part of my perception and awareness. I use Newoldkid, a double oxymoron identity, as an example, providing context for my unexpected journey into Haiku.

433. Between new and kid
Pristine old me discovered
Two oxymorons

A Haiku is a gestalt that starts as an inspiration, awe, vision, illumination, clarity, or a peak experience inspired by entangled unfolding moments, patterns, structures, forms, and emotional responses later translated and composed into a word-paintings of simplicity, surprise, humor, beauty, grace, love, and other unusual emotional experiences. The design processes juxtapose things, ideas, concepts, or images and connect through creativity, relationship, Apophenia, and Synesthesia. Another pattern captures unfolding brief moments, touched by clarity and nuances, and deleted by essential mental functions. It is an abstraction, integration, addition and deletion, simplification, and translation of insight, epiphany, or sensory perception of the ongoing event into words for self or shared. The reader reconstructs the moment and emotions, adding his personhood to supply the deleted nuances. It could also be a personal enjoyment of a product of an author. Experiencing and interpreting a Haiku is always subjective and the preferred social values.

A Haiku as a poem is an art created by conscious and unconscious intention and processes, using different mediums, subjects, styles, technics, and many levels of artistic mastery. Every individual will fit into a specific category and format. The medium is words, and a completed poem is a collage of words, images, feelings, emotions, abstracted relationships, and synthesis into a whole. There are strict formats, rules, styles, subjects, seasons, and so on, but all these evolve into different manifested forms.

222. An inspiration
Compose of words and feelings
A Haiku painting

Haiku as Memory

There is always a lag between an experience and writing a Haiku. The initial inspiration is recorded in memory and translated into words to create the poem. Many are distilled from memory and can also be composed of ideas, concepts, or brainstorming, letting creativity connect incompatible patterns and distantly related qualities without encountering things, events, or conditions. I had over 35 years of three days a week of solitude and communion with nature; and many authentic experiences of surprise, wow, awe, inspiration, connection with Thingies, unfolding interconnected moments, or just carefree living, in comfort, ease, and peace, which I call Experiential Haiku. Not everything is bliss or profound; the other patterns are sadness, suffering, misery, and the pathos of Humanness.

Without reading Haiku, the juxtaposition of images, sensory processes, and the break seemed natural when I wrote or read for myself. The writing is in the present, and memory is always a reconstruction as new. Every Haiku I write from memory opens a door in my mental warehouse and updates the experience. One reason I started writing a few regular poems in 1977 after a spontaneous transcendence is to have access to the specific, blissful event in daily life. Publishing was not an intention. But here I am, a newoldkid, in a writing marathon.

Haiku as a Creation

A Haiku is a synthesis of seemingly unrelated pieces of a living puzzle and, when completed, is a creation. It is a peanut comic strip in words. It can stand by itself for generations and be discovered, updated, and amalgamated to experience an aesthetic, personal, social, or spiritual moment. Some that use contextual conditions are only funny, silly, or absurd. While communing with nature, seasons, sensory awareness, perception, images, and emotions were the component of traditional Haiku, mental, symbolic, spiritual sensation, and discernment are examples of modern Haiku.

Three Components of Haiku

As an expanded experience of wholeness, Haiku is composed of three complex events. I arbitrarily divided it into three distinct conditions: The Experiential Haiku is a moment of illumination/connection; the poem is a translation, composition, still personal; and the Social or Shared Haiku for Others and the world.

The Experiential Haiku

The spectrum of experiential Haiku is an entire range of events/conditions that results in a wow, a woe, or the predominantly routine daily moments I call the Circle of Ecstasy(COE) when transformed into an awareness of subdued bliss, samadhi, joy or solemn sadness. I also defined these experiences as the Haiku that write themselves with intense emotional awareness and without words.

The Wow

We all experience an inspiration, insight, communion, and emotional response of awe, bliss, a joy that lasts forever, sweet-bittersweet, peaceful, or deeply touched. They can be from ordinary appreciation of nature to a moment of clarity; the ultimate is a fusion in Oneness with the PC, where awareness, bliss, and any creation or separateness cease to exist. When we are back in the material world and try to utter a word, we only emote wow, aah, oh, or a sense of magic, a miracle, or anything supernatural.

215. A wow experience
Writes by itself without words
A living Haiku

The Woe

The other extreme is sublime sadness, with many mixed emotions, including tears of joy, absurdity, laughter, or complete silence and stillness.

The two experiential Haiku above are opposites but share similar patterns, pure without mental abstraction when viewed in Wholeness. Capturing and translating these breakthrough moments and writing them into poems are generally called Haiku.

The Daily Routines

The routines and mundane are the endless daily living. Now, things and images that are the commonly accepted conventions can also initiate the emotional state of clarity, freshness, fusion or connection, and simplicity. They are invisible, symbolic processes and forms/structures that are more challenging to experience. They have weights and facilities as matter; they have spiritual functions and are readily available, possible, and bring about the same extraordinary events and feelings as a communion with nature in a specific season.

The wonder is multiple levels and layers of experience and emotions; the minimum is the default body, mind, soul(BMS) state of ease, comfort, calm, joy, and the mental/symbolic and the metaphysical/spiritual frames have their own Zen Isness, later condensed into a three-line format. It is a momentary escape from the imprisoning power of the senses into a higher-dimensional world.

The usual range of daily living is what I highlight as the predominant state of being in the COE. The extreme emotional wow is excellent, but the blissful mundane have the same unified experience, if not better, because of quantity and appreciation of the quality of emotions.

Haiku as a Poem

After an experiential, emotional event, a poet may translate the insight into a poem. It is a summary, interpretation, integration, and composition of a transcendence, abstracted through language into a written form, and when shared or read, presents an opportunity to recreate the same or close enough delight to the poet's intimate seeing, complemented by tone, gestures, timing, exaggerations, like a stand-up comedian or entertainment. In groups or reading, it offers social activities with various possible emotions, humor, play, and even sublime, religious, spiritual adventure, no longer restricted to the three-line-seventeen syllables. Once written, shared, or not, it becomes personal and social.

Social Haiku

The original Japanese Haiku was a social event, and a group of poets corroborated the poems. Publishing, reading, or sharing an author's inner world makes a personal invention into a group event. The words have to be familiar and easily understood by the group.

Humor, play, being concrete, innocent, a child or a beginner's mind, or just seeing things as-is are essential characteristics of the complex world of Haiku. It is common to observe higher intellect, mental and spiritual interpretation, meanings, images, and discerning hidden connections between juxtaposed conditions in sharing or reading Haiku to adults. But in traditional Japanese Haiku, direct experience of nature, Zen without abstraction, and humor were expected and valued. Young kids can easily be as straightforward about what their senses tell them, which often is challenging for adults.

The Leap

The leap is a complicated subject, and I can only try to make sense of it, being new to the genre with limited knowledge and experience. My immediate association is a bridge or a jump that results in an altered state, a fusion or communion with the Divine, accompanied by bliss or ecstasy. Like anything essential and experiential, a Haiku's goal must be defined. The ideal objectives are transcendence and happiness, but the range of experiences includes all variations of emotional states.

I know my SST's feelings, sensations, and states, but how do I translate them into words or language? For the poet, the leap is immediate and direct, while for the reader, it is distant and abstract. The two are encounters of different conditions and processes. The fundamental techniques and emotional responses towards Oneness are the same but also unique and subjective. It is like a dance, but individual moves, styles, and patterns are personal and improvised. Everyone is dancing and adding their spin to the experience. I assumed these processes, practices, and incidents apply to critical life events, religious raptures, and extraordinary happenings. God or the divine has infinite forms, functions, and processes. They may not even repeat despite apparent similarities.

232. Moments of wonder

Offspring inspiration source

Father of Haiku

We live in a symbolic world; words, symbols, and language are powerful. I used father because mothers are the given source. Fathers have offspring too. Fatherhood provides all parenting forms, much different from mothering except for love. They also come as inspirations, oohs, aahs, and transcendence, later delivered as Haiku babies.

The Mind Is in the Now

As a function, the mind is always in the present moment. However, the content can be the past, present, or future. Once brought to awareness, the past and the future all become the here, now, and current, including the higher dimension, unless the intellect and judgment strictly impose artificial time. The poet's choices, commentaries, criticism, and the purist bound by their dogmatic restrictions are okay as long as everyone is allowed freedom.

It is okay to form a group with precise rules and conditions and abide by their strict agreements. Once anybody insists on how things should be, especially by their bias, beliefs, or preference, we create a problem and impose our values on others. If anybody does not approve of a poet's way of writing a Haiku/poem, then change the channel or one's event, and maybe LOL at the stupidity of the poet. Then maybe you got through the hidden or deleted subtleties of the poet's moment and leap.

Use of Pronoun

I am partial to the personal, although much aware of the preference for the social or universal, removing the Self/ Ego. I don't see the Self as a problem, more than the motivation, intention, or goals. Valuing one over the other is an individual choice. Universal personhood was a choice I made to expand my wisdom after my first SST.

The use of pronouns is another vital issue. I freely use personal pronouns probably more than the Japanese Haiku poets, not only by intent but also by cultural and linguistic differences. Their culture may have a preference for avoiding personal pronouns. What is significant to me is the closest I can use words and symbolic representation of the candid moment in language. I am more than an observer but an active participant. Removing me is detaching a personal relationship created by the illumination or communion with nature or symbolic images. A significant chasm between using a pronoun and being the pronoun or stated in another way is back to an existential moment and a vast experience using words and language. I can be an empty boat, a boat, and a boat replica. I have less hesitation in using the personal pronoun and the reference to Self, probably because I differentiate between writing a poem for self or a limited group, in contrast to the original or traditional Haiku, as a social event, where reference to self is inappropriate or at least discouraged, and this may be cultural or because of the close connection between Zen and nature.

I assume readers will be free to use their new, direct personal emotions and insight. Poem interpretation is a reader's responsibility for their experience instead of duplicating or copying the poet's actual events. It is okay to evaluate the poet's intent, meaning, or state, but eventually, the reader's moments are the essential encounter with the abstracted facts/truth. Even when awe or wow touches our core and is shared, a social event ends in an inner world for all participants.

I ask the question: why remove the poet in the completed Haiku? A critic who promotes no poet's self-reference may be unable to get out of himself, be compassionate, and share the poet's joy, pain, or sorrow.

The Power of Deletions

Combining is a given process in every creation, but deletion is necessary for life, living, and social interactions. Creating and navigating in our symbolic world is impossible without simplification and integration. We will get bogged down in details in social interactions and relationships. Deletion is like breathing, and simplification is like the air we live in, unconscious and automatic. Whenever I use words or language, I know the necessary deletion process.

The editing process increases the deleted nuances, intimate dialects, emotions, and unnecessary details to polish the written form. The simplification is all good, as with the excess/personal are excluded---the face of God emerges.

Whether an event happened or not, or if only a myth, it is okay as long as it manifests the grace of the human spirit, causes awe and eternal joy, or connects with divine matters. Symbolic and spiritual conditions are processes and events that involve 3rd, 4th, or higher dimensions.

All epiphanies, transcendence, and breakthroughs to the divine are subjective, infinite, eternal, and accompanied by bliss or ecstasy, which one experiences moving in and out of Oneness, the divine, and the material world. These phenomena are an evolution in action, primarily spontaneous or serendipitous. They are more rigorous than the selective scientific method because all variables are considered, embedded, and intertwined.

Breakthrough may start as intention, attention, and mindfulness, but the Self must surrender. Awareness is the last paradoxical barrier before Oneness and needs temporary suspension. The way is a negation, dissolution, a lull of being here and now to the void, emptiness, and nothingness. What can also be majestic without deletion is an opportunity to add one's self moment, a new creation, discovery, and mine alone, fused forever with PC.

The significant struggles with the disconnect result from deleting many considered nonessential parts of the experience, which can vary from the poet's personhood, preferences, habits, and level of integration. For the reader, the process is meta-level to the poet's subjective state. The first thought or words are the correct words for the poet, described as a beginner's mind. Still, when a Haiku has to be shared or read in public, the first completed Haiku needs review and editing, and words still have to be precise. The context is social; others, the world, and words may need to consider or conform to the consensually validated cultural conditions.

Chapter I

The Physical Haiku World

The physical world is our immediate environment and ecosystem. The spirit took the human form, the sensory source of joy, and the awe of experiential Now—all a tiny wonder portion of creation. The communion with Nature is a seamless Haiku in motion.

Our senses constantly receive stimuli, and the experience with things around us often becomes the source of our inspiration to write a Haiku. The visual pattern is the more commonly used because the mind is outwardly focused, and the visual field in the present moment is instant programming. I am partial to images/visuals. My senses trigger a photo or a dialogue, and I get the completed transactions faster. I can see and hear a movie scene and get a complete understanding of the movie, sometimes even repeating a short conversation. The visual recall is more accessible, but I struggle to write them.

The poetry process is a way to revive our lost reverence and connection to Nature. Haiku is an excellent art form that makes us aware of encounters of all kinds and our emotional responses in daily activities. The counterparts of the material world are internal experiences, which are often symbolic representations of our earthly events.

Traditional and Seasons

6. The moon danced all night
Winter sky supplied the songs
Bright stars went ding dong

8. Persistent tweeting
A red-winged blackbird delights
A winter-spring day

19. Tranquil wildflowers
Rode the waves of autumn breeze
Synch beauty and grace

20. A young dogwood tree
Swayed, bowed to the thunderstorm
Youth cherished the wind

21. A lonely daisy
Caressed by tender raindrops
A radiant new bloom

29. Rain pours on sere ground

Raindrops by-passed ocean home
Slake Mother Earth's thirst

30. Snowflakes from heaven
Flutter gently to the field
Spread warm white blanket

31. Walking in the park
Cool breeze caressing my face
Awareness is bliss

41. Mindfully driving
Stop letting a squirrel go
Took a chance and crossed

45. Drifting snowflakes swirl
Blown giddy by a snowstorm
Stacked up all day long

46. Mountains' minds create
Brings Sisyphus' myth to life
All forms of rocks sprout

47. A teardrop from rain
Dangling in a blade of grass
Splash another grass

49. Birds soar up the sky
Flap their wings in casual grace
Their bliss of flight shared

55. Silent performance
Gentle unfolding actions
Rose petals blooming

64. The visiting rain
Played the roof like piano keys
Soothing me to sleep

65. An old quiet house
Built from materials of love
Never gets lonely

66. A bitter ice storm
Loads a tree to kiss the ground
Humility bow

74. Depressing Monday
Eerie windless silence
Darkness before storm

75. An aged birch tree
Dance gracefully with the storm
Knows young living well

78. The sun pours the heat
Melts the snow, and water drips
Winter's summer break

87. A patch of green grass
Enclosed by a window frame
A snapshot of sight

104. Beginning Ice storm
Cautious walk to get the mail
No delivery

106. Hi Mr. Firefly
Twinkle, twinkle in the dark

Happy you're in love

107. Departing winter
Sings a tearful goodbye song
Spring empathy bow

129. Backyard Evergreen
Never shed leaves in winter
Silent endurance

147. Springtime has arrived
Winter hibernated dreams
Out the cave alive

153. Shoveling packed snow
Back-breaking work in the cold
Aches and pains foretold

171. In a quiet stream
I tossed aside my troubles
The rains brought them back

Sufferings and joy go together, and you can't have one without the other. Life is a duality/polarity in the earthly realm. Hardships, obstacles, and troubles are shadows cast by light. Expand light perception and open judgment or love the shadow.

174. The sun fades away
Clouds instantly filled the space
Skyscape live paintings

175. Nature is friendly
No demanding self to please
Yields to selfless needs

189. Hesitant sunrise
Too many jobs to complete?
Want more time to sleep?

190. Wee purple flower
Why the gaze, coy look, and smile?
Ah, something is up!

191. Autumn leaves falling
A single tree reveals three
Divine space sharing

For many years, I admired and connected to a beautiful full-blown tree from a distance in summer. One late autumn, I was happily surprised and smiled; three separate trees formed a single tree, sharing the same space. Without mobility and freedom, they created a masterpiece of virtuous living and sharing.

For Shadow, a meek, silent black Labrador manifesting-love

> *192. Fireworks like cannons*
> *Firing in all directions*
> *Panicked Labrador*

> *193. Can't get off my eyes*
> *The moon dancing with the clouds*
> *Windy autumn night*

> *194. A glass of water*
> *Dreaming of easing one's thirst*
> *Nature fulfills dreams*

> *195. Forty-three winters*
> *Spring, summer, and autumn too*

196. A Daisy breakthrough
A crack on my backyard fence
Welcome, I'm Tony.

202. Surprise, surprises
The rain is the same elsewhere
Silly bucket list

209. A row of Black Ants
No testosterone workers
Loyal to the Queen

211. Wildflowers blooming
Posing, dancing, and laughing
Celebrating Spring

218. Clear sky, windless night,
The Worm Moon shines extra bright.
Tonight is daylight.

March 19, 2022, is a clear-sky night. It is the last day before Spring, and yesterday was the last winter full moon.

219. Last night of winter
Full moon behind the birch tree
Playing Peekaboo

221. Winter on deep sleep
Buds of trees wildly blooming
The first day of Spring

224. Hi, Mr. Squirrel
Happy to see you again
Still wary scanning

225. Thank you, Mr. Breeze
For setting my plants and trees
Their bending workout

231. Flashes of lightning
Thunderous earthquake warnings
Tornado nearby

Nature and matter are alive and mainly in a unified state. They have their moments and selfless intentions. When forces are in extreme polarity conditions, the gods and their infinite wisdom correct the extremes to settle in the middle. We may not be welcome, particularly when balancing the forces within their immediate universe. An example is: in a severe thunderstorm, an isolated tree may want you to stay away while connecting to the lightning-to-ground voltage. The lightning, thunder, and tree will send you vibes. Trust your instinct, feel the vibrations or the hairs in your skin standing, and get out of the way.

233. Clouds, the magician

Pulling tricks, scenes in the sky

Endless Rorschach test

The clouds are like little kids, playing, creating, improvising, trial and error, and discovering. The created scenes are Rorschach tests to check if you see anything in the sky or how is your unedited internal state of being.

236. A grass morning dew

Loves the death kiss of sunrise

Reincarnation

237. An irenic rose

Petals inhumanely plucked

247. A youthful Squirrel
Hopping on top of the fence
Has courage I lost

Bodily function is just one of the things you lose when you get old. However, for what you lose, you gain wisdom.

251. One-legged Seagull
Catches threw food in midair
No fun beach hunting

North Padre Island, a handicapped Seagull, hopped and struggled to keep up with the flock while feeding. It did better competing by flying. Nature adapting is a sight of grace.

270. Springtime in Japan
Cherry blossom paradise
Dagwood trees blooming

Dogwood, Redbud, Wild Plum, Bradford Pear, Fringetree, and others are flowering trees, which I call Springfield

Cherry Blossoms, and any of these trees can be an inspiration.

284. Ravens in my yard
First visit in twenty Springs
Four seasons good luck

285. In a single breath
Lovely Spring bloom quickly fades
Miss it in a blink

286. In a second breath
The late bloomers come along
Thank God for stragglers

298. Dead branches falling
Birch tree shedding winter clothes
Windy Spring morning

300. Recycling Center
Traffic jams of good-doers
Mother Earth smiling

311. Squirrel on the yard

Joined foraging by a crow
Cyclic pecking heads

317. Soaking the cool breeze
In my backyard paradise
Completes Bucket list!

319. The morning sunlight
Shines daylight in a Dew world
Little Prince's cosmos

328. Spring storm rage again
Birch tree wild swings falling limbs
Broken mental bones

350. A timid Acorn
Mustered the courage to bloom
Kinder boss the Spring

417. Spring blooms on both sides
A Turtle crosses the road
Ahead of the Hare

418. Lined by the roadside
Rainbow of Bougainvilleas
Love their daily toil

419. Driving home at night
Canadian geese block the road
Swerved and kept them safe

424. A lively old pond
Surface-covered yellow dust
Springtime allergy

Dandelions

143. Wild Dandelions
Nature has no word for weed
Man--- a weed killer

315. Alone Pink Tulip
Surrounded by perennials
Ecstatic Diva

316. Dandelion blooms

Besides diva pink Tulip

Auditioning role?

The following day, a Dandelion blooms beside the Tulip

401. Understudy thrived

A full bloom-shining diva

Dandelion clock

The Dandelion turned into a white Blowball. I was feeling like flying with the pappus as It blew away. It took several minutes for the wind to disperse the pappi. Each was hanging on or just wanted to stagger the dispersion.

402. Oh Dandelion

A meek innocence of ease

Heaven in a weed

I can commune with a Dandelion and be at peace. Maybe being labeled a Weed has something to do with it. It is an example of heaven in William Blakes's Auguries of Innocence's second poem line, "And a Heaven in a Wild Flower." The Circle of Ecstasy is ten default states of bliss that we all have but take for granted or, for many, are invisible.

After two weeks, the purple Columbine perennials in full bloom took over the Tulip and Dandelion's show.

Japanese Maple

I love my backyard, Japanese Maple. I planted it as a tiny tree, almost dead and damaged. I gave it a good spot and watched it over the years; we have silent chats and regular visual connections. I watched it grow very slowly. Over ten years, it has grown to the perfection of grace by mastering the grace of imperfection.

A Haiku is a record of a relationship with a thing. When an encounter remains a source of joy, a vision, or an inspiration, the level of connection or attachment increases, and several Haiku can come out of the experiences. Traveling to desired places for a bucket list to provide joy is a no-brainer, but having the same feelings for mundane or familiar routines is a more significant challenge. The rewards are enormous, and you already have conditions for delight without doing anything except awareness, appreciation, and gratitude.

145. Frequent dialogue

With a Japanese Maple
He thinks I'm crazy

146. Ten years of patience
A curved Japanese Maple
Mastered perfection

220. Japanese Maple
Woke up earlier this year
First chat before Spring

318. Japanese Maple
Request pruning dead branches
Senior Downsizing

Cars, Traffic, and Driving

The daily routine of automatic driving, ease, comfort, and successful intentions are constant sources of joy.

79. Driving in traffic
Orange light on the side mirror
Be alert and safe

80. Yellow parking marks
Line cars in protocoled space
Life of planned order

81. Green light is a go.
Red light is a stop command.
Yellow light---freedom.

A typical ending is to speed up and own karma choice. Traffic lights direct behavior for safety, but pick and freedom create their contextual events against the emotional indifference of karma.

82. Racing the Devil
An idiotic winning plan
The finish line—Hell

243. Driving leisurely
Drivers alert, smooth traffic
A routine of peace

258. Work zone
Nobody is slowing down

259. Driver texting
Crossed the median ditch
Car wrecked but safe

Temporary behavior change is for sure, but in the long run, for some, the dangers or risks taken are seldom modified by accidents.

Zumba

244. Crowded Zumba class
Nobody's wearing a mask
Social distancing

312. Beautiful ladies
Jello mass motion as one
Zumba paradise

423. Zumba room mirrors
Every Dancer's reflection
Duality Zen

434. Zumba on hand brake
No cardiovascular strain
Elegance and grace

435. Zumba on steroid
High cardiovascular stress
Ecstasy of pain

436. Zumba instructor
You know this is intense dance?
I'm a Newoldkid

437. Senior on front row
Gorgeous ladies on Zumba
Old man showing off

Covid-19 Pandemic

My wife's belongings are all our house's flora, fauna, and most knickknacks. While I communed with nature, she made nature homebound before the Covid pandemic. They were all discoveries for me. The funny thing was that they became another bridge that got us closer. Somehow, my belief/mantra of "Everything I get is love" unfolds in the most minor expected forms, a moment in time and space. The place is essential, but the relationship is the crucial component of the encounter, and we carry a symbolic representation of things wherever and whenever we need them. I relate to the homebound nature and artificial objects without distinguishing between the internal or outside environment, and the freshness of the present moment is distinctively layered.

132. Last year's four seasons
Observed and enjoyed at home
Covid confinement

133. Covid, Oh Covid
Why art thou tortured the world?
Show thy love and care.

I searched for and validated my belief that every creation is needed and has a reason for being. It is difficult to find beneficial things in horrendous situations or events. I have to go back to love, which I equate to PC.

134. Covid-19 masks
Simulacrum of safety
Danger depth disguise

135. Kissing and huggings
Victims of covid-19
All on life support

136. Covid benefits
Solitude and reflection
Shunned golden moments

137. Families and friends
Essential partners in life
Best Covid vaccines

138. Four seasons homebound
Nature, moon and stars followed
Keeping Covid out

223. Mandated to home
Every season moved inside
Nature reproduced

I can have all nature in symbolic forms to touch my inner core and be in communion with PC, adding oozing ecstasy of Thingies in a room.

299. Stimulus package

Evildoers gorge on dole

Heavens raining storms

323. Ceiling floodlights

Counting six moons

Covid -19

397. Air, land, sea travels

Covid-19 casualties

Born to a new life

Nature Homebound

The threat of sickness, hospitalization, and death from COVID-19 significantly changed the lives of the world's population. Social distancing, mask mandate, travel restrictions, group gatherings, and parties forced people into isolation. The resulting crisis in all aspects of living created stresses and uncertainties, and we lost many personal choices and freedom. Millions died, and families could not attend the funerals of loved ones. Kids who needed social contact with classmates were taking lessons on the internet. Depression and violence increased.

The Covid pandemic made it necessary to restrict at home. Four seasons, comfortable weather, and nature became natural and symbolic homebound. All in the immediate surroundings became a replica of the outside world. A home is an inner, intimate environment with some plants and flowers kept inside. A connection with personal things complemented communion with nature. The initial step was a struggle to find the typical relationship and pattern of very different environments, complicated by the familiarity of home.

The personification of thingies, which I have practiced for forty-five years, made it easier to form a relationship with natural and artificial flowers, plants, valued knickknacks, and belongings. The connection is a two-way street, regardless of equality and hierarchy, which I changed depending on existential needs.

The seasonal conditions are different from seventeenth-century poets. Modern life, with all the amenities of contemporary living, allows more seasonal and weather controls. The home environment is temperature preferred to Spring and Autumn and excluded the extremes of Summer and Winter, although they are available when we go outside.

There are always hidden benefits of even the most horrendous tragedies and disasters, but a pandemic of this magnitude is something we have never faced before. Discovering Haiku while on a homebound mandate is one of the numerous benefits I appreciate. I have never used Facebook or any social media before, being contended to be an old Dinosaur. I must leave my comfort zone and learn the standard technological progress.

I brought nature, the four seasons, and the outside world indoors. Another layer of discovered processes, patterns, forms, freshness, relationships, and emotional responses is similar to solitude in nature. Our home became a source of communion, newness, and inspiration for a Haiku. The home and things are too familiar, but once attention, personification, and context change, connecting with the objects around the house is more accessible. Nature brought indoors is a good replica of the outside. It is a reproduction in that you carry paradise/spirit with you, and the differentiation and separateness are mental and symbolic.

7. *Tick tock tick tock tick*
Pendulum swings back and forth
Grandfather Clock marks time

9. *A Doll on display*
Gazed, smiled, and winked discreetly.
Secretly, she's fine.

A tiny Doll in our curio cabinet on the living room corner, complete with souvenirs, knickknacks, and keepsakes

73. *Painting on the wall,*
Claims the best spot as a prize.
Beauty is its pass.

77. *A loaf of french bread*
Toasting in an air fryer

A taste of Vienna

83. Row of mixed orchids
Aesthetic elite army
Guarding the window

85. Cheese on the table
Endures the cut of a knife
Pain, service and love

86. Running Ceiling Fan
Pull the hot ceiling air down
Warm comfort and ease

88. Walking in the house
Functions, processes and things
Haiku everywhere

90. Sitting relaxing
Entangled in miracles
Mindfulness---needless

91. Gazing without thoughts

A corner slice of a room
Oozing Haiku bliss

94. A house's living room
One thousand chameleon gods
Playing hide and seek

Symbolic/abstract words create images and emotional responses in the Now. Haiku are everywhere.

105. Steaming hot coffee
Waiting for it to cool down
The telephone rings

109. A pantry handle
Turn on her seductive charm
Stomach growl---tempting

110. Refrigerator door
Mosaic forms and places
A collage of bucket list

Tours, bucket lists, and vacations in paradise provide opportunities for newness by doing things never done. Still, the critical and challenging task is to experience the novelty of the familiar and be awake. The mind is never lazy, but simplification is well-developed for efficiency and convenience.

118. Ms. Moringa
Don't be afraid of winter
Our love will keep us warm

My wife cares for all the flowers inside our home. Ms. Moringa is my care, and I seasonally move her inside the house.

131. Loud TV Commercial
Distressed the ears and mind
Peddling needless stuff

140. Brewing fresh coffee
Sets the tone and aroma
The glee of desire

141. A pair of sandals
To give an older man ride
Waiting at the stairs

142. Old Rice Cooker
Tummy boiling 2, 4, 6
Burping rice-water mix

144. Light switch I envy
Turns darkness into daylight
Heartless clarity

158. Old books on the shelf
Outdated forms by Youtube
Dinosaur Seniors

160. TV took a rest
Worn out working long hours
Went to sleep early

162. Sunlight got homebound
Captured by suspended dust
Countless friendly ghosts

177. Relaxed and musing
What to write for a Haiku
Bullpen on a cup

178. Lamp on the table
Meek and humble as a lamb
Master of Darkness

183. Snake plant on a pot
Assessed very carefully
No threat to safety

185. Magic Money Tree
Cash harvested each morning
Best financial gift

186. Plastic centerpiece
Inventing lies to impress
A Social Climber

187. Dedicated friend
Caring for my mess and waste
Faithful garbage can

Ordinary things around the house are always available to teach humility, acceptance, connections, love, and compassion. Having no Self-made is simple.

200. Family picture
Imprisoned nostalgic past
Genie's three wishes

230. Passing by the room
Thingies around pondering
A friend or a foe?

246. A working wall clock
Staring at my eyes
Asking me the time

Someone unaware of their power, talent, and internal strength looks outside.

248. Things in my attic
Students of Rip Van Winkle
Missed twenty-one Springs

249. Tall powered speakers
Screeching highs growling low tones
Getting drunk on songs

250. Tore up my bedroom
Looking for my reading glass
Napping in my head

253. An old spider plant
Spinning cobweb in my heart
Trapping only love

306. My bed seems to care
More now than ten years ago
Hugs, my body frame

307. The dust on the rug
Contented gathering moss
Vacuum cleaner's joy

309. Blue eye souvenir
Bought in Turkey for defense
Home safe and healthy

I am traveling back to Europe at my refrigerator door. The blue or evil eye is supposed to help and is one of the many magnets attached to the refrigerator.

310. A dull slicer knife
Pile of crushed ripe tomatoes
Bull in China Shop

321. Sandals at the stairs
Nature and places homebound
Basho's trips indoors

The covid pandemic made daily life homebound, an opportunity to discover the beauty and grace of the ordinary.

330. If only
I'm a cat
Nine suitable Orchids

336. Sword plant by the door
Sharp ready for a battle
Samurai warrior

351. Hot air from the vent
Mirrored by curtain movements
Winter never left

Chapter II

Mental Haiku World

Haiku is a symbolic universe with infinite and eternal potential, possibilities, probabilities, and opportunities. It is a physical, symbolic, and spiritual world populated by diverse races, people with various cultures and languages, and many individuals, each with unique personhood.

The mental world, the reification of the soul, the translation of moments, and the integration of the web of life are a bit of living. A haiku is an aesthetic-designed art synthesizing rhythmic patterns, context, and meanings to be shared and enjoyed.

Sensory images and perception, particularly visuals, were the everyday inspirations of the traditional Japanese Haiku poets. It has evolved, and modern poets have the freedom to expand, experiment, and create new forms, subjects, contents, and processes.

The mind is the 6th sense organ with mental sensory and perception capabilities similar to the physical senses. The inspiration, wow, and composition are biological, psychological, and spiritual.

In the material world, the myth is often more influential than a factual event, and that power can spread to many more than the truth limited to the person who had the possibility.

In the higher dimension, where time and space are beyond the material world, there may be no difference because a particular is universal in Oneness. The essential process is to know the context and the realm of the experience when one is in the differential analytical process of discernment and separateness. Clarity of choices becomes a better option.

Haiku is heavy on the need for intellect, imagination, and mental processing. The brevity maximizes deletions and the gaps of disjointed unfolding processes and moments. The poet's culture, language, and country may present additional obstacles, as reported by translators of Japanese Haiku.

History of the genre showed that social events and humor played a significant role. Reading and understanding the meanings of some Haiku is a major challenge for some who can not make the connection between the images or patterns. Some require more than a leap. I wonder whether that's the poet's aim. I guess anonymity and distance are the same as the internet provides in our times, and intentions are harder to discern. Sometimes I smile or get puzzled. Maybe the poet is putting us on, or the joke is on me. What is lovely is that all ranges of emotional responses are available, and I always choose love or humor and accept absurdities. All humor has an element of aggression, so I watch the punch line and deflect or laugh at it.

Mental Haiku

28. Bonded polar pair
Unified mirror feedbacks
Change dreamers beware

34. Sail on
Ocean garbage
Fulfill your dreams

48. Regrets breed regrets
Mistaken mistake, a fault
Double miseries

50. Person to person
Relationship with parents
Ends parent-child roles

A significant milestone in life is to break the parent-child roles and have a person-to-person relationship with their parents.

56. Unspoken love song
Disjointed love limericks
Two unpaired bookends

69. Creativity
Unites the soul of chaos
Graceful solutions

71. A relationship
Embedded in love and pain
Lives eternally

72. Less and less to none
Accumulating nothing
Masters abundance

92. Wicked intentions
Prolific society weeds
Hideous human deeds

93. Senses are thresholds
Pathway to the inner world
Gatekeeper the mind

96. A kindred group meet
Gossip, laugh, cry together,
A symphony show

100. Removed excesses
The face of beauty reveals

God has rough edges

102. Imagination
Tales confined to virtuous life
God handles the rest

103. Greek mythology
Majestic, imperfect Gods
Absurd humanness

108. Cobwebs in my brain
Memory threads left behind
Traps woes all the time

113. Water I drank
Swallowed me entirely
Owned every cell of me

128. Fears, doubts, unknowns
Paralyzed choice and duality
Moments of freedom

130. One thousand rocks

Turn over without God
Nowhere as promised

139. Left-hand dominant
In a right-handed world
Upside down insights

199. All of yesterday
Four seasons constant repeat
Permanence is real

204. Thingies everywhere
Just being the way they are
Is all that's needed

207. Walking and breathing
The steps and breaths sang a song
Nature died laughing

208. Effortless walking
Silence, comfort and no thoughts
Countless miracles

212. Subtitle on screen

The ears made dispensable

Eyes learning to hear

I trained myself in Synesthesia by practicing and allowing the multiple interchanges of sensory perception. Examples are hearing colors, seeing sounds, etc. The training gave me several layers and access to experience the world. Poetry uses synesthesia and apophenia besides metaphors, similes, and figures of speech.

216. We are deluded.

All that I receive is love.

Psychosis is bliss!

The mind only knows what has gone through the rigorous differential analysis, judgment, certainty, and action. The emotional response is factual and the truth. It involves complex, well-verified mental and symbolic processes. The secret is to enjoy the bliss of self-illusion/delusion without taking anything seriously or sharing it with the world.

217. The soul took man's form

To know fleeting bliss and woe

The human spirit

252. Please leave me alone
Pleaded the distant mountain
Your thoughts are painful

255. Freezing rain in spring
A bitter taste of winter
Old habits spoil dreams

256. Totally pitch black
Darkness afraid of the dark
Predators looming

257. A Robin in spring
Pecking its window image
Selfish with no self

263. Inspiring visions
Imagination on gear
Apophenia links

272. Two sides of a coin
Third side of peaks and valleys
Weather, weather life

314.Apophenia
Daily practiced by the mind
Judicious the heart

322 Lovely Chocolate
Bogus sugar substitute
Senses psychosis.

Confused senses, agitated mind, tricked judgment, and confusing emotions result from artificial chemicals mimicking the desired sensation at the expense of BMS unity. The benefits of trickery to obtain desires are destructive to the spirit and will manifest a corresponding karmic load.

327. Warehouse in my mind
Litters of gems trash joy woe
Lifetime of sorting

344. Senses
Imprison us
Incarnate form

346. Order or chaos
Extreme edges to breakthrough
Genius or madness

Like inventing, you go through several prototypes, verifying the best solution. I include the extremes to maximize options and allow for serendipity. Knowing the 5-7-5 format was enough information to jump into the trial and error. Little preconceived notions give me more freedom to create. I like a blank canvas to paint. It is more challenging, but whatever I learn or unlearn are discoveries, and they stay with me.

353. Hanged my peace prayers
On drifting bucket list clouds
Ukraine angel rains

354. Modern Dictators
Brutal abuse of power
Ruthless genocide

355. Working on top floors
Delusion of heaven
Administrators

420. Lonely Loneliness

Paid a visit on my walk

It wants company.

421. Things image vision

Juxtaposition hints

Apophenia leaps

Haiku is two or more physical, mental, and spiritual Thingies or patterns, connected by disjointed links to breaking the differentiation of senses and the material world and being in Oneness with PC; Eternal Ecstasy flows. The goal is to revert to default primordial BMS before the incarnation and learned humanness, accumulated matter, beliefs, and experiences.

Eyes

51. Eyes are cameras

Taking selfies of the world

Stored inside the soul

52. Eyes are clear windows

In this house, we call the soul

Peek and see a god

Mirrors

63. My kind twin brother

Living in every mirror

Always says---love you

The mirror can be a therapist, an altered self, a reflection of you, or the opposite harsh self. The choice is a path to bliss.

201. My mean twin brother

Living in chosen mirrors

Reflexive bitching

My other twin brother I saw when I was younger. I haven't seen him since I quit visiting the mirrors where he lives. Maybe he is avoiding me because we no longer do bitching, or the mirrors where he stays are broken and discarded.

76. Painful emotions

Criticisms change notions

Critics are mirrors

440. Critics, the mirrors

Reflections of social norms
Choose well---be not torn

Critics, editors, reviewers, and anyone providing feedback or criticisms of our work are mirrors. Mirrors have personalities and can give us all variations of reflections, reassurance, validation, or devastating effects. Motivation, intention, context, and the nature of the relationship beyond neutral are essential to either help or hurt us.

Light

111. Death
A constant shadow after birth
The light---Life

112. Light portrayed
Gray shadow on the sidewalk
Dark-Self-portrait of all

A Fleeting Moment

156. Boston Ferns by the corner
Enticing multiple stairs
Tiny me could climb them

The first layer of perception and awareness, Boston Fern, was the staircases and provided a silly wish.

157. Miniaturized me

Out-of-body experience

Scaling Boston Fern

I had a flash of miniatured me scaling a Boston Fern---an eternity play and an altered state of minor bliss.

403 and 404 came out of a glance, similar to the above #157 Boston Fern Haiku. A small visual field of mangoes pastel art on the wall, close to a brass doorknob, drew my awareness. I was put in a trance by a previous gaze of wonder at a Japanese Maple in our backyard. I know everyone had similar special experiential moments, and Haiku followed later.

Verbal communication has disadvantages and difficulties in getting the message across. The space, time, context, and realm of encounters define their usefulness. Some apply the appropriate method to the proper person or crowds.

403. An old brass doorknob

Bright and proud as it can be

Fool's gold, but happy

Modern life is enamored with plastic and imitations. Authentic faux is funny, but it satisfies desires and gives momentary joy, which may be eternal for some.

Oscar Wilde posited that life imitates art more than art imitates life. Nature and art let you experience the perfection of imperfection and the imperfection of perfection.

A Haibun: What Does a Mystic Know?

What does a mystic know about a layman's woes? He declares the truth in the spiritual booth, a higher symbolic dimensional globe. An ordinary man knows the reality of an illusion of matter. To follow the mystic, who lives in the stratosphere, is to negate the physical world and to put one's life in peril of bodily injury, suffering, and death. The life of the mystic contrast with the ordinary man's world, but he suffers the illusion of an illusion. Communicating with different contexts and meanings frequently happen in a social encounter, and one wonders how we avoid confusion and still understand each other. A snake bites its tail to destroy itself, and a layperson has to contend with the senses and perception in the material world.

67. A mystic proclaims
The world is an illusion
A snake bites its tail

Another assertion, even more severe, regarding delusions, but to be sure, the mystic has to contend with the senses and perception in the spiritual world; he has to accept the reality of illusions and fantasies; otherwise, he suffers the karma of his beliefs and choices. Is the mystic serious or putting us on?

68. A mystic asserts
Delusional all humans
Question not---He's nuts

Chapter III

Spiritual Haiku World

The Spiritual World, the eternal/infinite soul, the first manifestation of Consciousness, the North Star of the mind, and the essence of one thousand deaths are a small portion of PC. The spirit is the vision and inspiration of a Haiku.

Art of any genre is life and unfolding, sometimes translated into words, paintings, story, or play. The translation expands an event into patterns and forms, meta-level distant from the sensory or physical experiences. The abstraction, simplification, and symbolism are higher dimension realms, not necessarily better than the experience. There is no difference between the BMS and what the differentiating mind constructs or conjures. The experience is seamless in three realms of harmony. Otherwise, any activity is discontinuous by constant buffering of data. The action and motion are in limbo, waiting and frozen in manufactured time. We are always living in all dimensions. The higher dimensions are only invisible because of sensory perception and processing of the mind, which is defaulted to maintain safety in the material world.

Paradise is a state of being within you and wherever you go. Yes, some real places are Eden, but look again. They are out there, and that pattern keeps you away from the silence/stillness of Oneness within you. The paradise you are, you make the rain or the sunshine, the bliss or the woe. Every Spirit took the human form for many unknown reasons, but for me, one reason is to create a personal circle of ecstasy.

Litany of Perfection

I listed this litany of perfection in the eighties while integrating the duality range, BMS—three layers of context, experience, and discerning the subtle differences between the ideal and the bad. I was redefining my valuation and judgment. The perfections were boundary guides on the aesthetic side, but by declaring them, we activate the other polarity end. Everyone in the state has a personal context, point of view, preference, or bias, and anyone forms their guide. The list is never comprehensive, and I do not claim expertise or truthfulness; everyone has their litany of perfection and imperfection.

The litany is a symbolic, spiritual, or higher dimensional pattern, metaphor in life, or a bridge to leap in creating a Haiku. The other bridge foundation is the Zen moment in the material world, nature, or the third dimension. Capturing both the momentary and the eternal is essential in writing a successful Haiku.

Adult, perfect servant
Aged, perfect sunset
Ancestor, perfect legacy

Body, perfect harmony
Breath, perfect balance
Buddha, perfect human
Change, perfect constant
Chaos, perfect novelty
Circle, perfect path
Compassion, perfect communion
Conception, perfect transition
Consciousness, perfect awareness
Cycle, perfect process
Death, perfect fear
Devil, perfect evil
Dying, perfect opportunity
Earth, perfect mother
Equilibrium, perfect health
Emptiness, perfect transcendence
Energy, perfect source
Enlightened, perfect wisdom
Evil, perfect violation
Fear, perfect stress
Gift, perfect gratitude
God, perfect love
Hate, perfect suffering
Heaven, perfect reward
Hell, perfect punishment
Here, perfect place
Human, perfect absurdity
Infant, perfect honesty
Impermanence, perfect change
Jesus, perfect example
Life, perfect gift
Love, perfect relationship
Marriage, perfect struggle

Man, perfect experiment
Mind, perfect evolution
Mindfulness, perfect task
Newborn, perfect spontaneity
Nirvana, perfect trap
Nobody, perfect somebody
Nothing, perfect absence
Nothingness, perfect beginning
Now, perfect time
Permanence, perfect illusion
Self, perfect delusion
Silence, perfect communication
Solitude, perfect isolation
Somebody, perfect nobody
Soul, perfect peace
Stillness, perfect motion
Sun, perfect father
Tao, perfect way
Time, perfect urgency
Universe, perfect creation
Void, perfect space
Water, perfect model
Woman, perfect form

Spiritual Haiku

1. Self wakes sun, earth wind
Life celebrated with joy
Bliss on every breath

2. Self smiles at the moon
Each heartbeat is ecstasy
The night is Eden

I wrote my first two Haiku to share in our University of Santo Tomas, Medical Class 1971, the Centennial graduates. I had no plan to write more, but four days later, six poems came to me, and they kept coming.

4. Life is ecstasy.
Everything is meant to be.
Fear died early death.

5. A land of bliss---Earth
Ecstasy is everywhere.
Perception hides it

12. A random kindness
Whenever done, ripples on
Whoever needed

14. Evil intentions
Ego sharpens sleaziness

Soul indeed is damned

15. Selfless intentions
Love service and compassion
Soul's guided actions

16. Ungodly desires
Devil's meticulous traps
Hell's celebrating

17. Power, fortune, fame
Forceful false gods to worship
Sad trade for the soul

84. Seeking solitude
Loneliness to emptiness
Hermit's Soul-itude

Desired solitude is bliss; forced avoidance of people is pain and suffering.

89. Present moment
Unfolding ease and peace

Earthly paradise

148. Alone reflecting
Heartbeat, breath, thought, and action
Divine miracles

172. Flawed spiritual texts
Source of needless pain and woe
God hides behind words

188. Hate being in crowds?
Design and carry your cave
Always a Hermit

198. Sitting motionless
Lost in silence, peace, and bliss
Only oohs and aahs!

254. Thank you x 3
Thank you x 2
Thank you x 1

In the material world, three is enough.

In the mental world, two is enough.
In the spiritual world, one is enough.
On the PC, zero/silence is enough.

260. Press release
April fools day
Devil's temptations

267. Famous dead folks' truth
Spin-off to sinister lies
Evil man's weapon

Dead people can tell the worse lies. We can't go back to the horse's mouth to verify it.

268. A popular myth
Is more potent than the truth
Faithfuls kill for it

Transcendence translated by intelligent people can become a myth or a dogma, mistaking the symbols for the truth, the divine, or God. We can be fanatics.

352. Loving intentions

Tossed to Collective Unconscious
The Source finds the need

356. A gratitude bow
Expressed without intention
Heaven's debts erased

357. Any selfless smile
Set the inner world aflame
Spread wildfires of love

358. Gloomy Spring morning
Endless forms of changing clouds
God's finger paintings

359. Friend's healing prayers
Whispered in perfect silence
God grants the request

360. Paralyzed lady
Vending rice cakes and desserts
Subtle divine vibes

Lucid Dreaming

37. Lucidly dreaming
A thousand desires fulfilled
Countless ecstasies

57. Dreaming with God
Angels and devils swap roles
Joy and woe switch poles

179. Frying omelet
A frog jumps into the pan
Woke up from a dream

241. I am flying
Walking at the ocean bottom
Dreaming I was God

The simplest things I did in lucid dreaming. The difficult ones are aggression, violence, and fighting evil. Our soul travels to all dimensions in our sleep, amending and unifying the web of life. If life is but a dream, as the song goes: the sooner I wake up, the sooner I dream.

242. Savoring French Fries
Three hours still on cloud-nine
Too slow---no can do

Fast-food restaurants are no place to dillydally, let alone be in a trance, but in lucid dreaming; there are no limits. The divine has eternity and infinity and has no default preference unless needed in the physical world.

Zen Buddhist Catholic Practice

One of my responses to who I am is: I am a Zen Buddhist, Catholic, doctor, and layman. All religions have the same fundamental beliefs, and I don't find any conflict in my practice. Zen is communion with nature/simple life; Janus-faced Buddhism is to experience both ecstasies and let suffering unfold and virtuous Catholic life.

297. Zen wonder moments
Love and compassion of Christ
Buddhist joy or woe

Zen

My take on Zen is awareness without awareness, Primordial BMS in Pure Consciousness, a single focus on a task or multiple tasks, meditation in every living moment in silence and stillness, noise and movement, joy and sorrow.

Zen prefers and values direct experience without abstraction or translation. The IS is the idealized event, a truth, and a truism as the minimum a person has to experience in the material world. But, a person's world is more complex than one can imagine. The mental, symbolic, divine, and spiritual realms are seamless concurrent moments of existence. The senses and perception are primarily for managing the matter or 3rd dimension, and their restrictive, even imprisoning influences are unfailingly hidden. Continuous transformation and integration into a whole of actual multilevel moments happen. The synthesis varies for each person, age, mastery, and state of being.

If one keeps silent, still, with no thought and no internal discourse, then the event and emotions remain fresh, minimally but necessarily modified by the mind. It is then a symbolic replica, no longer the actual event. The essential criteria for translation and simplification are close to the facts/truth for clarity and symbolic representation. Mastery of language becomes a skill, limiting or increasing the replication. The distinction may be moot because BMS, by default, are unified. Reflection and study make a massive difference because the event discerns the differences and maximizes separateness and mental differential analysis. As for me, I only get concerned when I have to define the different realms of the experiential Now; otherwise, actual/direct, mental/symbolic, and even spiritual have the same potential and possibility of ecstasy or suffering as I choose.

Master and Student

The question of dependency is a critical component of the master-student relationship, which is helpful, wanted, and necessary for children up to 27-35 years old. A differential hierarchy, dependent roles, and guidance are created that eventually must be transcended or given up.

Dr. Maurice Bucke, in his 1900 book "Cosmic Consciousness," studied the history of mystics who had transcendence. Twenty-five to thirty-five is the most common age of rebirth. He also predicted that mystical experiences would be more common and that we are moving to higher consciousness, which is now an ordinary happening.

Once an adult stops asking for answers to doubts, uncertainties, fears, unknown, metaphoric absurdities in life, living, being, and accepting all consequences, he is free. After all, the master is another human, challenged to the trappings of mortal life and living necessities. Mystics, Saints, Gurus, Masters, Priests, persons who had Near Death Experiences (NDE), or any being who broke through to the divine world and came back with knowledge and wisdom and made the radical and irreversible transformation of beliefs and being will be susceptible to fall out of grace. What is invisible is that everyone has a moment of clarity, grace, and enlightenment. Nobody is permanently enlightened. We all move in and out of enlightened moments.

After 30 years, rebirth is a milestone in taking responsibility for living one's life—no excuses or blaming but responsible for every conscious or unconscious choice, intention, and action. Rebirth includes regaining the lost childhood innocence and bliss of being, but now with the safety or survival threats internalized and an overhanging consciousness that constantly monitors safety. We are socialized, develop a Self, and internalize beliefs, habits, and experiences of our culture and species. A child is full of spiritual life, seeks bliss, is unafraid of consequences, and borrows intentions and safety measures from caretakers or parents, which a child incorporates into the development of Self and becomes a member of society.

438. Personal keyboard
Consigned to everybody
Endless bad karma

The rebirth process can be spontaneous, instantaneous, or commonly during crises, stress, trauma, serious problem of BMS, any form of suffering, or NDE. It can also be gradual through disciplined self-reflection, meditation, study, getting a guru, or any purification of Self by a complete or radical transformation of humanness and practice of virtuous life. There are infinite ways to be reborn, and light is a commonly reported variable. Any rebirth or Transcendence is a new journey to unpeel the layers of learned humanness for the update, revamp, and massive change in personhood. It is a liberating process, accompanied by many epiphanies, discoveries, and layers of subtle and blissful ecstasies.

Zen Moments

In between these words, process, moment, thought, idea, and form is a gap/rest/emptiness and nothingness.

119. You are present, here, now
One thousand now, here, present
Are present, here, now

120. Zen is Now, Here, Present
An Isness, that is, Is
An experiential God

121. Zen is.
Zen is, Is.
Zen is, is, is

Zen is--a process; is Is--a being/thingie and is, is, is--are unfolding moments.

122. Zen is Now.
Zen is Here.
Zen is present.

All three are in an earthly world where Now is time; here is a place; the present is an action.

Consciousness Between Moments

123. Zen Present
Awareness, Mindfulness
Present Zen

124. Zen Now
Emptiness, Nothingness
Now Zen

125. Zen Fusion
aa, bb...yy, zz
Dissolution Zen

126. End
Gap Zen bliss
Start

127. Stop

Rest Zen clarity
Go

271. Zen moments warehouse
Museum of tragedies
Odd friends in my heart

408. Bliss in a dot
The sound of one hand clapping
Minimalist life

Buddhism

I live both agony and ecstasy of Buddhism, although both processes occur in the natural polarity cycle. Nobody escapes necessary suffering, but Nobody escapes joyful life too. The predominant experience is joy and comfort, except for people with severe physical or medical conditions, mental illness, or broken spirit. Our mind makes the distinction and judgment towards preferential expertise and emotion.

154. Buddhas earthly lives
Many never leave a footprint
The universe keeps tally

155. Buddhas come and go
Many are nobodies
The gods know them all

95. Life is suffering
Living is an ecstasy
Janus-faced Buddhism

197. Life is suffering
Buddha's truth--the other truth:
Life is ecstasy

304. Janus-laced lingo
Translation misconceptions
Faux visions of God

338. Living
I'm no empty boat
I'm sorry

341. Now
I bear witness

Catholicism

Christ's ways are virtuous life, suffering, and compassion, to name a few, which are also Buddhist teachings. One doesn't have to be a martyr. The Renaissance and The Reformation already narrowed the distance between God and us.

229. Why claim a sinner?
Go through Christ's crucifixion
Believe you're redeemed

337. Being
I offended thee
Forgive me

339. Here
I failed thee
Please, one more chance

340. Present

I bow
Divine thee

342. A moment
Thy presence
I'm grateful

343. Offer your other cheek
Surrounded by freaks
Follower of Christ

349. Easter egg hunting
Discovery in hatched egg
Christ's resurrection

Chapter IV

Emotional Haiku World

Emotion is the endpoint of human activities, intentions, or actions. The mental component of the experience and the translation into words to form a Haiku is never possible without the mind. There are very few actions related to the senses that are direct experiences. All sensory functions are input to the reason for further integration. Ideas, metaphors, onomatopoeia, the leap, and apophenia can create events that result in bliss, ecstasy, and joy.

Kids process Haiku less with the concept of leaping, requiring complex intellect, imagination, mental symbolism, and abstraction. What you see, hear, or unfold interaction is what you get fresh, immediately, without being pretentious. For adults, the challenge is to regain the childlike innocence the BMS encounter, write about the happenings and share them.

The Emotional World, the karma of intention, the result of the action, and the valuation of judgment are the cosmic portion of ecstasy. A Haiku leap gives a feeling of bliss and delight. It is the mental equivalent of experiential joy when one communion with nature, objects, or events in the material world.

All feelings of pleasure or happiness are the target emotional states. Inspiration, writing, or reading a poem creates an emotional response, and the natural reactions are a range of joy, sadness, or neutrality, depending upon valuation. Still, what is preferred is that joyful extremes are sought while sorrowful extremes are avoided, yet both may be the cutting edge for complicated passionate responses and experiences.

Emotional Haiku

313. Are roses red?

Can't violets be blue?

It's okay; I love you.

326. Falling in love is

An eternal ecstasy

In infinite Now

329. Oh, what a tough choice!

A dozen gorgeous Roses

Want to dance Haiku

335. No discoveries

Checked my pulse three times over

I'm alive, still dead

400. Steel Magnolia tree

A retirement living gift

Peace service lives on

The pain of love, compassion or any selfless virtuous action is a healthy form of sharing and communion with another being.

Bitter-Sweet Discoveries

My emphasis here is strong, mixed, or blended emotions and feelings of discovery.

308. Bitter-bitter-sweet

Other side, bitter-sweet-sweet

Emotional coin

Happenings that trigger these paradoxical emotional states are everyday extraordinary Zen moments but are often fleeting, avoided illogical and non-desirable experiences. The mind is protective of the Self and helps us navigate this unwanted time bubble by separating the two-sided emotional coin to favor the preferential value, norm, or belief. A child, beginner, or creation's mind at conception will not need protection, but the adult/Ego mind does.

The socialized mind is misguided in over-protection. We miss a whole world of the unusual expression of love. The third side of the coin is the glue that binds the two sides, and this is love manifested in an entangled relationship. These patterns are examples of confusing things, experiences, and emotions that I lump into metaphoric absurdities.

This emotional coin is a word representation equivalent to a Yin Yang, a cross-section of a wave. The conjunctions are the connecting links and the third side of a coin, joy and, or, with, but, and so on--woe.

These conditions populate the two-sided coin in the physical, mental, spiritual, and emotional country and will be sources of Haiku experiences and poems.

18. Loving Compassion

A bittersweet masquerade

Pain, woe, and delight

Bittersweet is a uniquely human experience. The word is self-explanatory. It bridges duality/polarity, allowing opposite emotions, usually joy and sadness, to blend.

60. All betrayal forms

Dump aches to a broken heart

Trust again and heal

116. Loneliness, what thou knows

More than isolation and pain?

Are you a part of love?

149. Ugly the beautiful
Oxymoron cast aside
A hidden path to bliss

Play

180. God plays Hide-and-Seek
Hiding in obvious places
He loves to be found

176. Haikuing haiku
All senses on red alert
Haiku haikuing!

181. Phonetic word games
Moonday, Chooseday, When-isday
Things action and time

I played word games with my grandkids and used phonetics to create images, visions, conditions, etc. Kids have no problem playing silly games. We used the days of the week and laughed at the funny things we imagined and sometimes provided context for activities.

Holding a box and asking grandkids

182. What is in the box?
Opened: empty--nothingness
God is everywhere!

238. Walking hand in hand
Lolo, do you speak Spanish?
Gar gor gir gor gar

Lolo(Grandpa) continued in a sing-song demeanor: "Si Senor, Kabayong Sarol, nung nukarin ka miragsa, karin ka mibangon." Translation: "A working horse must stand up where it falls."

I was eight years old, visiting my maternal grandparents and walking in their yard. I was impressed and in awe and kept the feelings forever in my heart. When recalled, the freshness is always new. Kids are impressionable and remember delightful or tragic moments.

239. Our speaking bird says
Padag, padag, pwak
Tony baba!

The second line words are without translation, while baba means to get down. The bird would repeat the phrases many times a day, and our family got a kick out of it every time. When it died, I was sad for a long while. The made-up words have emotional equivalents rather than word meanings. I have expanded and still use the pattern.

Baby Danica

58. Thunderous laughter
A carefree child refreshes
A long-lost childhood

347. Two-month-old infant
Giggling from silly faces
A guru of bliss

348. The first infant smile
Parent's delightful journey
Child's angelic world

Fishing

22. A shad-scaled crankbait
Burn it faster and faster
Bang! desire attained

23. Spook topwater lure
Walked the dog slow, kaboom! Missed?
Got you---second strike!

24. Crawfish-colored jig
Gently crawled the lake bottom
Thump! a thrill of tug

25. Big white spinnerbait
Steadily pulled medium speed
Wham! I set the hook

26. Tranquil blue-bird sky
A post storm fisherman's guide
Leary fish won't bite

264. Swimming school of bass
Every fish that bites my lure
Knot in my joy net

265. Jigging silver spoon
A pissed-off bass in the boat
Hello and goodbye

266. Hairs flapping frenzied
Boat running sixty-seven
Grandson laughing wild

269. Sunny day fishing
One thousand casts with no bite
The sun is biting

302. Saltwater fishing box
All the hooks are rusted
Caught fish had tetanus

53 Years of Marriage

114. I need
More than a lifetime
To love you.

While asleep without waking her

115. Progressive tenderness
Three affectionate kisses
Each, a lifetime of love

432. My wife's tone of voice
Makes me plunge a dagger
In my heart.

Tears

Tears appear the same, but the triggers, emotions, and experiences have a wide range and depth. The context or the event can quickly distinguish between reflex and emotional tear response. An example is shedding tears and cutting onions, which often brings laughter.

117. Freshly sliced onion
Hurting yet forgives the knife
Reflex tears laughing

59. Rivulets of tears
Flowing down a smiling face
Magic trick of love

Tears of Gratitude

240. Mother opens the car door
Giggling baby talk with her child
I cried

I have witnessed and even participated in similar lovely events but never cried. I'm in paradise, so I thought, but after some searching, I realized that I have been watching the news daily, praying for peace for the children and people suffering from wars and disasters, but more so by what we do to each other. I didn't know I had been carrying this sadness for three weeks. I did not have to stay in my car, but God wanted Me there. The scene somehow released the trapped sorrows in my heart, opened my eyes, and connected my tears and the manifested love for a fleeting bittersweet gift. I was grateful.

Gift Giving/Receiving

205. You are the other

It's okay to be selfless

Be compassionate

206. The other is you

It's okay to be selfish

Accept and be grateful

425. A friend

In need

Compassion pain

426. A friend

I need

Love hurts

Sequoia National Park Tour - April 21, 2022

Basho and some early haiku poets traveled much to explore new territories and discover unfamiliar Nature. Without the convenience of modern technology, travel was most likely rigid and slow, but it provided opportunities for meditation, reflection, communion with nature, and writing poems.

Yosemite has to wait. A severe snowstorm diverted our trip to Sequoia Park; an unplanned bonus visit erased one item on my bucket list.

361. Storm diverted tour
Sequoia National Park
Delightful surprise

362. Fast Kaweah stream
Caressing every boulder
A boulder my heart

A fleeting vision of a continuous rushing stream of rough-tenderness carves a massive boulder to aesthetic smoothness. The boulder and my heart became one.

363. Baby waterfall
Leaping vociferous flow
Radiant confidence

364. Climbing winding roads
Accepts dizziness and risks
Fairtrade for desires

365. Every Sequoia
Ancestor's identity
Met them all today

366. Straight stretched Sequoias
Slows down, touching the heavens
Every tree gets blessed

367. Sherman Sequoia
One thousand wisdom-earned years
Nature's divine gift

368. Unlike Mutt and Jeff
Snapshots with huge Sequoias
Giant and small chics

369. Sequoia's burn scars
Eons of malformations
Perfect imperfections

370. Sierra Nevada Crest
Luzon's Cordillera peaks
East-West symmetry

371. Miles of orchard trees
Uniformed differences
Monotonous grace

373. Munching an orange
Vision of orchard workers
Grateful for each bite

374. Snow on mountain peaks
Melting migrating neighbors
New friends met downstream

Yosemite National Park Tour

First Day - April 22, 2022

375. Sunshine finally
Slick spots to Yosemite
Careful slow driving

376. Snowballs beat the car
Random fireworks snow splashes

Two cannonballs bangs

Falling wet snow peppered our car windshield, one baseball-size scary bang, one football-size louder boom, and instantaneous screams. I can't believe the windshield didn't shatter. Good karma!

377. Severe late snowstorm
Snow-covered Yosemite
White Christmas in spring

378. Yosemite Valley
Eyes can't contain the marvels
Only breathless sigh

We entered through the tunnel, and the first stop was El Capitan. What a moment! With one glance, a monolith with a mist on top, two massive protruding peaks on the right, and the Horsetail Fall, our group entered a magical world--- two altered states of enchanted days.

379. High, low waterfalls
Cut granite walls in tandem
Upright river flows

380. Colossal Sequoias
Monolith after monolith
Puny experienced

381. Way cool way
Is a way cool place to stay
Yosemite trip

Second Day - April 23, 2022

382. Press releases
Are motivated statements
Peril if believed

383. Born a spirit
Live humanness
Die peacefully

384. I am an expert
I know a little bit more
I am dangerous

385. Numerous black snakes

Warning poisonous and risks

Mountain winding roads

386. Biggest and tallest

Sequoia and Redwood trees

Live in the same place

Fantastic, they both live in California. They claim their title, respecting each other. The massive ones are tree monoliths; the tallest are giants. Both give people an experience of ecstatic joy for their size, presence, and beauty and a feeling of pleasure puny with one's smallness.

387. Gliding small blackbird

Touch down softly in a field

Choppy jet landing

Every part of Nature is a unified sensor. Man's creation is a poor copy with limited sensors.

388. Boulders on both sides

Marks the paths of a long trail

Safety Boundaries

389. Old log by the trail
Lonely counting passing folks
We became close friends

The climb on the Mist trail towards Vernal and Nevada Falls is stiff. I frequently stopped and made friends with old logs and boulders along the sides. I discovered lively ecosystems among the logs. Each log exudes a history, characteristics, and personality, making resting easy, comfortable, and joyful.

398. Rapids river falls
Waterfalls of rivulets
Blend in a calm pool

The loud sounds of powerful rapids capture attention, and on the side are small waterfalls where water moves and drops slowly. They all meet again in a calm pool ahead—a vision of a family with kids doing their playing and reuniting later.

399. Brown Bear with purpose
Unperturbed by the joyful crowd
No threats to tourists

On the way home, the group was lucky to encounter a big brown bear about 60 yards away. Lots of cars stopped, and folks took their best pictures. A wildlife encounter was a bonus.

Fresno, California - April 24, 2022

391. Farm specialty store
Mega bloom white roses fence
Beauty Monolith

392. Rush to the airport
Flight canceled due to fierce storm
No forthcoming flights

393. Driving to LA
Speeding to join the gridlock
Plan C is on board

394. Wild spring storm again
Terror I have been before
Deja vu nightmare

395. Radiating sunlight
Exultation deja vu
Routine Spring morning

I had both experiences, and the present storm activates the
event in actual time or dreams. Duality often cycles in the
Now, helping to balance, harmonize or update memories.

396. Colorful food trucks
Ten ethnic cuisine pageant
Pay and eat to judge

A luxury of options becomes a struggle of choice and a
good problem. I had a taste of dinner in paradise and
judged nicely.

Chapter V

Circle of Ecstasy

Over the years, I integrated my Zen/Buddhist/Catholic/ Doctor/layman's life into ordinary ways of living. Life is seamlessly unified by PC and Oneness but artificially separated by the senses, intentions, and the mind. How do you communicate and highlight the simple miracles of daily life that everyone goes through? The mysteries of the universe and the vast majority of the creation are supposed to be overwhelmingly complex and unknowable. The alternative I did to minimize lucid confusion was 35 years of selective silence and stillness, focusing on unfolding moments, valuing functions and processes as soul patterns until I identified the invisible predominant ease and joy of living. About ten years ago, I came out of my inner world/ solitude and started sharing my SST expressed in mundane events and conditions of experiential moments. While our perceptions, intentions, actions, and realities need no explanations, defining or translating our experience into symbolic, metaphysical, and spiritual context to be able to share is challenging. Approximation, deletion, metaphors, mastery, and so on are helpful, yet still limited or unable to capture the essence of everyday transcendence beyond concrete/static phenomena. The English language can translate complex and spiritual events, but it is a struggle for me. Telling how it is, sounds unbelievable or an exaggeration.

The awe, certainty, and extraordinary processes shared as truths, even when expressed in humility, are often perceived by others as silly, absurd, or arrogant. Sometimes I challenge ideas, ideologies, and dogmas by using neutral judgment, passing them through mental duality/polarity filters, and studying how they play in daily life. I am friends with these forms: illusion, delusion, and the true nature of reality. Even without understanding, I trust the processes I go through more than my abilities to translate the unfolding events. Simplification and abstraction delete the beauty/ugly nuances. Otherwise, we meet the devil in too many details, but God is into even more in circumstances that make the eternal minute infinite. Some gifted individuals can consist of the deletions and come close enough to report the original experience. Others have mastery of language and can add invisible details between words or sentences. There are readers or people spoken to who intuitively fill in the blanks and come out of the encounter richer than the simplified version. The emotional valence can either be good or bad, depending on judgment, and is always personal and subjective.

I get drawn to the undervalued, non-preferred, adverse polarity conditions, routines, mundane things, and events that happen without intention but make our lives comfortable and a thousand seamless Nows unfold. I lived them as meditations in motion and actions or default states to fall back on when the mind is agitated.

Satori/Samadhi/Transcendence

1977-78, I had three spontaneous SST, with sunlight, darkness, and clouds, accompanied by ecstasy and channeled unknowable truths. When you break through into the divine, you take information, knowledge, wisdom, and facts when you return, and a radical change in your entire being occurs.

My way to SST was from happiness to a state of Oneness/ecstasy and paradise instead of the shared path from suffering, NDE, and tragedy to joy, wisdom, and peace.

97. Sunlight captures me

A communion of spirit

Paradise regained

There was an explosion of light. In a tiny moment, an irreversible transformation of my being, a conveyance of eternity and eternal life

98. Draw in the darkness

A fusion of disguised light

Self in a new world

There was intense Suchness. Infinity and abundance are Zero; nothingness, emptiness, and void are sufficient; less than less is enough. PC provides everything needed.

Two grayish formless clouds have been in my awareness for two days and suddenly fused on my drive home from work. An ecstatic feeling accompanied the rebirth.

Circle of Ecstasy - Oneness

The COE is ever-present in earthly time, eternal time, and infinite space, without beginning and end. Initially, the COE is a daily intention, mantra, or ritual to awareness, appreciation, and gratitude until they become the default state of ease, peace, and happiness. The repetition differentiates awareness into ten invisible joyful states, incorporates eternal and infinite higher dimensions in understanding, and makes the 6th sense active with the five senses. Unconsciously or mindfully, I fall back on to rest, relax, and communion in silence and stillness; each moment can be a joy that lasts forever. I aim for the default primordial BMS at conception before any learned humanness. Still, from senior to birth, BMS is more challenging and provides the opportunity to discover infinite/eternal earthly blissful moments better than the primordial state; otherwise, what is the point of the spirit taking on a human form?

Oneness is silence.

Silence is ease.

Ease is comfort.

Comfort is harmony.

Harmony is calmness.

Calmness is peace.

Peace is Paradise.

Paradise is bliss.

Bliss is stillness.

Stillness is Oneness.

The next ten Haiku represent each state of COE and to fall back on and take a moment of peace.

283. Silence is my name

Stillness is my steady game

Oneness is my aim

273. Rest and be quiet

And feel the presence of God

Between the letters

274. Mindlessly walking
More and more walking, walking
Great pleasure of ease

275. Sitting without thoughts
Sitting, more and more sitting
Delights of comfort

276. Body, mind, and soul
Seamlessly functioning whole
Joy of harmony

277. The world went to pot
Smiling, nothing but smiling
The inner calmness

278. Enemies all gone
The devil is an ally
No more war but peace

279. The mundane routines
Invisible miracles
Earthly Paradise

280. Afterlife Eden
Agonies of Hell and fire
Conundrum of bliss

281. There is a stillness
Longing to discover you
A falling raindrop

Every raindrop is alive and has stillness. We avoid rain and have neglected our reverence, grace, love, and gratitude relating to nature. It's mind-boggling; a raindrop is just one of God's infinite creations to break through beyond humanness.

282. Mountain will not move
Become one with the mountain
Oneness always moves

Tell the mountain to move; it will not move. Request the mountain to move; it may move. Oneness has perfect motion and perfect silence, present in all creation.

I have kept mantras, rituals, and guides of silence and stillness for many years.

be silent
any thought, a jumbled word
any word misses the point
any speech misunderstood

be still
any motion, a commotion
any activity, an agitation
any action, an intention

after a breakthrough

be lucidly confuse
be awkwardly cool
be in paradise
eternally and infinitely
blissful

Oneness is impossible to keep permanently. Thoughts, desires, and intentions always break into BMS and the humanness of matter. The human condition is a COE and a Circle of Suffering(COS). Life is suffering, as the Buddha said, but the normal state of Being is happiness and Peace.

In my Catholic ways, the rosary metaphor helps focus on a state of being in earthly time, or one after another, without any particular sequence and repeating, combining eternity and infinity. In artificial time, quantity is crucial, but in endless time, one is enough. My fallback preference is silence and stillness. By default, the original body, mind, and souls are harmonious and Oneness.

Each COE condition is put in the repeated eternity/infinity awareness and context of all dimensions of existence and experienced in the physical world. The mind, however, makes the distinction and focuses on the priority of matter and safety; thereby, the higher dimensional experiences are restricted. It is a battle to balance the social conditioning of desires and the Self.

287. Eternal

Infinite

Oneness

288. Eternal

Infinite

Silence

289. Eternal

Infinite

Ease

290. Eternal
Infinite
Comfort

291. Eternal
Infinite
Harmony

292. Eternal
Infinite
Calmness

293. Eternal
Infinite
Peace

294. Eternal
Infinite
Paradise

295. Eternal
Infinite
Bliss

Circle of Suffering

Separateness/Incompleteness

The COS is the ten counterpart pattern and the close antonym of the COE. The First Noble Truth in Buddhism is "Life is suffering," the fundamental nature of life. However, I emphasize that life is bliss, happiness, or ecstasy. Joy is the normal state of being more than suffering. The criteria I used is the mundane default state of being as detailed in the COE. These states are unconscious, initially, as awareness focuses on safety, survival, daily tasks, and intentions. Awareness can be directed to COE until they become necessary daily tasks, habits, and appreciated. It is essential to be mindful of these routines or to fall back on them to calm oneself. They can be mantras, rituals, or daily affirmations. I used the conditions in the circle as moments of gratitude in ordinary, mental, psychological, religious, or spiritual presentations, highlighting the higher dimensions. I have no quarrels with anyone and agree with what is mainly promoted by experts. Still, I see infinite ways to bliss and the evolution of habits that make life easy, comfortable, and delightful as an essential part of most daily living. I value simple life, the mundane, ease, harmony, peace, silence, and stillness, and I pay gratitude to them. However, the mind gravitates to COS when desires, wants, and intentions fail, and conditions are miserable. I commonly associate Thoughts with Noise, and use awareness when it unfolds.

.

Separateness is noise.

Noise is disturbance.

Disturbance is discomfort.

Discomfort is disharmony.

Disharmony is discord.

Discord is distress.

Distress is Hell.

Hell is misery.

Misery is turmoil.

Turmoil is Separateness.

Primordial/Pure Consciousness

One of the channeled wisdom and truths on my first SST was about PC. My closest symbolic representation of PC as a necessary way to communicate is to divide PC into the positive creation/separateness side of the matter and the negative/dissolution of matter into Oneness. The infinite/ eternal ecstasy/bliss comes in the dissolution or suspension of the mind and the physical senses and the fusion with PC, moving in and out of the mental priority for the third dimension or material world.

32. Total Potentiality
Total Possibility
Total Probability

Triad of PC manifested to creation, Separateness, and matter. It is a positive representation of PC.

33. Formlessness
Emptiness
Nothingness

Triad of PC manifested by separateness, dissolution of matter into the void. It is the negative representation of PC. The two triads are complementary, like a mirror image.

Oneness

10. Unscrupulous thoughts
Broke the stillness of Oneness
Born was suffering

11. Empty mind, no thoughts

Ego took a vacation
Nothingness is joy

13. The physical world
Separateness perception
Matter illusions

27. Life is eternal
Transcendence beings we are
Fear not death and woe

35. Absolute darkness
Everlasting emptiness
Secret door to bliss

There are two parts to the above PC triads. The door to Oneness is infinite, but the path where differentiated matter dissolves to be Oneness is the common pathway. The pattern is commonly fusion for creation or back to the material world. Moving in and out of fusion and dissolution is a joy that lasts forever.

39. Silence, stillness peace
Consciousness permeates in all
Equanimity

40. Pondering choices
Karma demands acceptance
All consequences

42. Communion with God
Desire agitates the mind
Togetherness torn

43. Oneness with The Source
A thought intrudes awareness
Joy or woe begins

44. Silence ease comfort
Harmony, calmness, peace bliss
Ecstasies of Self

53. Mind is mysterious
Consciousness, creation, life
Weaved in unity

54. Ecstasy is now
Eagerly waiting to share

The Self hesitates

61. Ease comfort and calm
Endless daily routines
Be the bliss they are

62. The sound of heartbeats
Rarely touched by awareness
The heart always knows

The heart is a vital organ, critical in maintaining life more immediately than breath, yet less focused for meditation. It is capable of multiple perceptions.

70. Incredible day
Endless ease, calm peace, and bliss
Not a jiff to miss

101. Cryptic Emptiness
Stillness between end and go
Nothingness is God

150. Forty years of work

Transformed the bliss of Oneness
To daily routines.

151. The personal
Is the universal
That is personal.

152. The universal
Is the personal
That is universal

In PC, there is no differentiation between personal or universal. In the physical world, one can start in either state and end in Oneness. We are all complete, a whole, in all dimensional realms, despite what our senses and mind make us believe. There is no need to copy, no worry to be copied; only need to choose peace and bliss.

159. Alternating steps
Lost in the gap of a Now
Bliss from there to here

Homeostasis is unconscious ease, comfort, harmony, and joy.

161. Rest myself in bed
Blanket sweet, warm and cozy
Silence, the moments

163. A pause or a gap,
Verbal snapshot of stillness
A perfect motion

164. No sound word or thought
A screenshot of emptiness
A photo of God

165. Sitting in a trance
A thousand Haiku waiting
Not Now

166. Image place feeling
Endless moments of Suchness
Sublime word collage

167. Questions, seeking, yearning
God plays Hide-and-Seek
I hide too!

168. In the moment
Separateness, duality died
Oneness

169. A blink of an eye
Infinite discoveries
A Beginner's Mind

170. Today's sufferings
Tomorrow's jubilations
No time in God's home

173. Fixed Enlightenment
A false god of permanence
Oasis mirage

184. You want ecstasy?
Eden is you, within you,
Be present here now.

203. Emptiness, nothingness
Are the pause, stop, rest, gap, space

Where God exists and waiting!

Every in-between unfolding process is a gap/rest/space of emptiness and nothingness where the PC is waiting. Be mindful, silent, still, receptive, and ready to give up awareness to be in Oneness.

210. Thingies are living
Harmoniously in nature
To share life and peace

213. Don't follow me
I'm lucidly confused
I'm heading nowhere

226. Creation separateness
Dissolution nothingness
Life cycle of a moment

Oneness is to the creation of the material world, while dissolution is toward Oneness in the higher dimensional world.

227. As my soul comes down

The Earth quickly got lighter
Problems float and fly

Earthly life problems have the power to weigh and wear us down. A little truth or guidance from the spirit coming down to the material world and mind always helps.

228. Perfect solitude
Perfect communication
Oneness with The Source

262. Ooh, aah, and aha!
An experiential moment
Of eternal joy

301. Graveyard of parents
Butterflies on two shoulders
Mom and Dad's presence

We were visiting our parent's grave, and at the start of our prayers, as if on cue, one butterfly alighted on my shoulder and the other on One of my sisters. They flew away after several minutes when we completed our prayers---a profound presence of Mom and Dad.

303. Infinite kindness
Dedicated to a Self
Virtuous way to peace

320. Every breath breathes
Every heartbeat beats
Is, is Is!

Abstraction, mentation, and disconnect are everyday mental activities and functions, but making the leap and connecting is difficult. However, mindfully or unconsciously, the COE is the default state of body, mind, and spirit. Although they have a terrible rap, we can depend on these conditions. A low IQ is okay; it is all you need in Paradise.

324. Life is suffering
Smile and listen to Buddha
Life is suffering

325. Earth is a land of bliss
LOL, listen to me
Earth is a land of bliss

331. Eternity
In a moment
Infinite love

Consciousness to Creation/ Separateness

332. Zero is enough
One is more than sufficient
Two is man's desire

Creation to Consciousness/Emptiness

333. Possibilities
One was first manifested
Two is universe

334. Self, a delusion
Universe is illusion
Nothingness is real

409. Still
Silent

A temporal moment in earth time is an eternal moment in PC and vice versa. An incident, event, or experience is an infinite linear forward, continuous reflexive feedback captured clearly by the senses and made invisible by the socialized/adult/Ego mind. The three above are examples of a cross-section of a wave/energy, represented by yin yang, to see PC in the universe/creation.

410. Noise

Distress

Suffering

411. Bliss-sadness

Misery-joy

Go together

427. Every little ease

Every moment of comfort

Our God-given gifts

428. Every harmony

Every minute of calmness

Our eternal joy

429. Every sense of peace
  Every experience of bliss
  Our paradise won

430. Every kept silence
  Every second of stillness
  Our Oneness fulfilled

Chapter VI

Haiku World After Four Months

The personal that may be universal is one I studied in sought solitude for 35 years, without reading or studying spiritual texts, religions, or seeking a spiritual guide. Desired isolation came naturally; one goal was emptying the trappings of the socialized Self and being in communion with a thousand unfolding Now. I wanted my direct experience to depend on my inner world/being. I did not want to go where the others had gone or expect from other examples or reports. I own my encounter or for poem interpretation, used my filters and personhood, and added nuances to the poet's message and deletions. Everyone has a lens through which to see the world. The lens and the experiential processes are accurate and fundamentally subjective. I shared my ways as a piece of my life's journey, and the user determines their choices and experience. I am delighted if any pattern resonates or assists anyone's well-being.

84. Seeking solitude

Loneliness to emptiness

Hermit's Soul-itude

It didn't take long for me to answer my Haiku evolution and learn that enormous texts, knowledge, rules, poets, and masters are available. Still, I follow maximum freedom, and modern Haiku does not have to restrict the 5-7-5 of traditional Japanese format and the seasons. But this came after I had written over a hundred of the 5-7-5 configurations before reading anything about the subject. As an afterthought, I better read and familiarize myself with the rules and practice. I also noted that my early Haiku was on past, mental, symbolic, spiritual patterns, contents, and memories, and less on the Zen-like present, here, now, which I have done in years of solitude. Yet, a room is oozing with COE. The gap/pause/rest, boredom, and no thought are tiny moments; PC is most available to communion in Oneness. It is a process that starts with awareness and, thru negation, into the Formlessness, Emptiness, and Nothingness of PC. Awareness is the last barrier to a breakthrough.

I am just scratching the surface of what has been out there, written, done, the mastery, creativity, and courage to experiment with new forms. I am humbled and overwhelmed by the beauty, brevity, elegance, clarity, complexity, and mastery of language by the mystics, masters, and poets. I have serendipitously entered another Earthly world of paradise and bliss. I can spend a lifetime discovering, learning, and encountering infinite manifestations of PC.

36. Keep silent and still
Mother Earth whispers love songs

A variation of the second line, which I used in Catholicism, is: Jesus Christ whispers love songs, and another is: God always whispers love songs.

Shared Haiku

Another history page was in Japan; Haiku, writings, and creation were public events. I write for me, trusting free association, unedited emotions and feelings, subjective experiences, and not a prescription for others to follow. I am a shy, private person and value my preference for solitude. I like discovering and improvising as I go along on complicated subjects without definite, consensually validated answers. If I want a depth study, I do it much later.

Once I considered sharing Haiku, I had to edit painstakingly, looking at the precise word that would resonate with the consensually validated reality of the culture, the symbolic world, and the smoothness of rhythm, flow, and tone. I knew the feelings and the original words, but the editing was problematic. The brevity and the 17 syllables format were like being put in a crucible, pressured to discipline and conform to the rules. Once I complied and learned the art, the hardships became the benefits. I realized that sharing all layers of the events has tremendous merits and exponentially expands. It becomes a creation for a social event. The poet's joy, leap, and peak experience remained in addition to the collective benefits that give a person or group of participants inspiration, laughter, and happiness.

Translation

Mystical experiences are spiritual encounters with the divine. Without being written, spoken, and interpreted remains as is and in the spirit. Once translated into words, ideas, or language, the reification process alters the essential element, and somehow, the soul/God often slips away. The worst consequences are creations of dogmas we use to destroy others with different principles. A monotheistic God is a significant cause of religious wars. Any other God is a threat to my God and my survival. Love and compassion have limited chances.

304. Janus-laced lingo

Translation misconceptions

Faux visions of God

Personification

Personification is to accept an insight that things are conscious and Nature is alive. Animals have minds and survival instincts that make them have intentions. Some can design tools. Unlike man's unlimited wants, natural laws define their conditions and activities.

Acceptance, humility, tolerance, forgiveness, love, and compassion are qualities the personification of the virtues allows to teach us to learn and experience. In 1977, I broke down the hierarchy and personified the things around me so I could relate to them. Breaking down the scale up or down is a much-guarded barrier to cross. We put our God at an unreachable height, making communion impossible. Maybe existential encounters of personification with Thingies paradoxically break our artificial distance from God. God does not need adoration and has no needs and wants but accepts and provides for everything.

Haiku Structure

Haiku is commonly composed of two juxtaposed images, things, or symbolic forms. They are connected, complimentary in a relationship, or even tenuously, but essential. One is often discernible, and the others may or may not be things, plus the poet is a participant/observer. The emotional component is ubiquitous, and using personal pronouns sometimes is necessary to define entangled relationships of all involved without exclusive referential to matter. However, in the original Haiku, there is an expectation that the poet's inclusion is minimal or excluded.

The poet's range of awe, woe, insight, enlightenment, bliss, magic, divinity, and so on to the freshness of natural activities are what Haiku is trying to capture and impart to the reader. Translation, simplification, and language make the task challenging, compounded by every poet's personal response and responsibility. However, there are times when a successful Haiku can convey and create a similar original poet's delightful experience or insight.

The original themes of Nature, seasons, and season words are still commonly used, but present poets have much freedom and choice. Yet, even Basho, Issa, Buson, and Shiki broke the 17-syllable form.

Restriction to the Classic Structure

Rules never hinder creativity. The regulations encourage discipline and discover elegant solutions within the defined boundaries. The invention can pursue the best solution when it is beyond the rules. The mind needs constraints or challenges to discern the basic patterns within or outside familiar outdated solutions. Verification and validations are necessary to conclude that they are better and more functional under complicated problems.

I am glad the modern evolution is progressive, and poets have experimented with the forms, subjects, and contents without seasonal reference. The images, objects, nature, creation, and context, as well as the Haiku and poets, evolve. The poets can use creativity and follow where spirits and emotions lead.

Gifts of Creation

The choice is defined when certainty arrives, but nothing is permanent; a sure thing is never in the bag—what a fantastic human condition. Uncertainty, random events, karma, luck, and fate are always a part of living. Certainty and predictable outcomes may be better for the body, but they put the mind to sleep and the soul to death. Creation never guarantees certainty; a more significant gift is potentiality, possibility, and probability.

214. Fried Cod on a plate

On the way to the stomach

Falls to the table

The Mind as a Sense Organ

The senses are the doors to our inner world. They are gateways, inadvertently separating the human/material, mental/symbolic, and metaphysical/spiritual worlds. The senses are the easiest ways to bliss, and without doing anything, ease, comfort, and seamless living occur.

The mind is the 6th sense organ with all the characteristics of the physical senses. It is the most complex sensory organ of perception and experience. It adds an exponential increase in functions and forms, not necessarily conflictual with the body functions. The mind differentiates, integrates, manages the BMS, and expands the levels and layers of available and created realities and ecstasies.

The evolution of Haiku to the current time validates the need for all variations restricted by the past. Three lines with minor numbers of syllables are excellent progress. A poet or a group can define the preference or their agreed criteria.

What Am I Doing Here Again?

Moving on, I accepted myself into the Haiku World, looking forward to experiencing other infinite, eternal wow and woe, composing Haiku to share. Endless discovery, eternal bliss, and keeping a pre-conception or beginner's mind are a blast. I must learn about this territory, the different cultures, art, and processes, with a long history, traditions, evolution, and many vital poets and masters to meet and experience. Encountering the ordinary, daily routine and anything there that no longer triggers excitement or changes in the senses are the crucial welcomed struggles of everyday life.

I have to pay more attention to tone, rhythm, and flow like a song, without depending on rhyming and strict syllable counts. I give myself more freedom to the over-the-line limit, but I have to see what happens. There is no loss of vitality and creativity with whatever restrictions and rules. Accepted or not, I plan to walk into this Haiku territory. I am in awe about rediscovering the ordinary and too familiar things, most especially about myself when I can have communion with the outside world. The essential element is the built relationship needed for love to be shared.

Next Chapter

The common wisdom is to have new experiences; some are radical changes, and others are too ordinary and invisible. The discovery, reflection, and appreciation follow later, after clarity, verification, and validation of broad emotional responses of joy, peace, sadness, and love.

I didn't realize I had another rebirth, my third childhood after my second one at 31 years old. The first was physical birth, the second was to regain childhood innocence, and this one was the integration and the harmony of BMS, child/adult/senior, and the corresponding emotions.

390. A discovery

Discovered discovering

Subtleties of Now

Subtleties and intimate encounters with nature, processes, forms, and mental/symbolic/spiritual equivalents are temporal/permanent, fleeting/eternal, zero/infinite layers of ecstatic communion or Oneness. The COE made the meeting familiar, simplified by the senses and social mind. Applying Yin/Yang, East/West, and receptive patterns helped make the connection.

I have already written a lot more Haiku, and in the future may write freely, using the modern format, content, and subjects, and even try the smallest number of syllables.

412. Again

Oh God

Service

413. Now

Lord

Love

I had accumulated enough Haiku moments and never intended to write them until now. I welcome and prefer minimal precondition information, and I look forward to what will happen.

I will make many mistakes, break some rules, and be criticized by experts, poets, purists, and turf defenders, which is okay. Like any new journey, familiarity is a luxury; doubts and stupidity hopefully lead to wisdom.

439. Success from mistakes

Gives new meaning to failures
Unforeseen wisdom

Nevertheless, oh, what blissful problems to face! Brevity, freshness, open fields to travel, and busy times are welcome opportunities. My joy can't contain my eagerness and vice-versa. Thank God for my COE. Indeed, it will help me.

414. Not enough hours
In a single day
For discoveries